Praise for

DEAD GIRL CAMEO

" 'I wanted to resurrect the girl,' writes m. mick powell in the introduction to this wonderfully collaged collection of elegies and found text. The poems that unfold are formally vast, ranging from abecedarian to contrapuntal to cento, studded with perfect little jewels of looking, of feeling, of deep knowing. These poems haunt, and celebrate, and mourn, and, to borrow the poet's own language, invent 'other words for gold.' I adore this book, and I look forward to seeing its work in the world."

—SAFIA ELHILLO, author of *Girls That Never Die*

"An orchestra of tenderness marks the brilliance of this book. mick is a star."

—CAMONGHNE FELIX, author of *Dyscalculia*

" 'All I know is when I see her, I'm certain there's a Heaven / somewhere, someplace, where it didn't have to end this way.' *Dead Girl Cameo* is not only an interrogation of the way society and celebrity culture fails girls, particularly those who are Black and queer; it is also a generous imagining of the lives that are possible when girlhood is protected and tended to. powell's incisive use of persona and form force the reader to reconsider our perceptions of icons such as Whitney Houston, Lisa 'Left Eye' Lopes, and Billie Holiday, while her evocative lyric asks us to examine our own longings, desires, friendships, and relationship to intimacy. This magical, knowing collection implicates both speaker and reader: In what ways have we robbed someone of their girlhood? Of possibility? Of desire? *Dead Girl Cameo* is a stunning debut, a call to curiosity, tenderness, and dreaming, a necessary archive that asks, 'Would you let me hold the memory?'"

—BRITTANY ROGERS, author of *Good Dress*

"*Dead Girl Cameo* is a revelation, returning pounds of flesh to our fallen icons with a lyric pulse strong enough to resurrect. Its pages reach through the mycelial network of Black queer girlhood, recovering the fugitive eros of their lives. Full of expert formal play and thrilling collisions with the archive, m. mick powell's brilliant debut is a gift to the living and gone, a righteous correction to the cultural record, and a tender elegy for all the girls we once and never were."

—KEMI ALABI, author of *Against Heaven*

"m. mick powell's gorgeous debut poetry collection highlights the devastating conundrum of many famous and beloved Black singers. Though they led highly publicized lives, powell's poems reveal that these women were, in some ways, ghosts while they were living. Bulldozed by the misogynistic music industry, abuse, and crippling societal expectations, Whitney Houston, Aaliyah, Billie Holiday, Lisa 'Left Eye' Lopes, and others were essentially making cameos in what should have been their leading roles. Through an innovative blend of queer feminist theory, collage, and docupoetics, powell pens a gorgeous elegy to some of our greats and revives them in perpetuity by countering their life's violence with a love that is pure, queer, and infinite."

—TAYLOR BYAS, PHD, author of
I Done Clicked My Heels Three Times

"*Dead Girl Cameo* stitches many tender odes, counternarratives, and snapshots of Black girlhood—from the violence to the beauty of it—into the warmest protective quilt for its subjects. Every single poem radiates such care, love, and craft that I was left breathless, unable to stop reading until the end. Interview snippets and headlines from the archives spotlight the voices and stories of the stars Aaliyah, Whitney, and others, yes, but powell's precision, wit, and sensuality make their own voice shine as a rising literary star. powell's formal and lyrical prowess make *Dead Girl Cameo* a propulsive and genius debut that I'll never stop thinking about."

—JAE NICHELLE, author of *God Themselves*

DEAD GIRL CAMEO

■ DEAD GIRL CAMEO

A LOVE SONG IN POEMS

m. mick powell

ONE WORLD

new york

One World
An imprint of Random House
A division of Penguin Random House LLC
1745 Broadway, New York, NY 10019
oneworldlit.com
penguinrandomhouse.com

A One World Trade Paperback Original

Grateful acknowledgment is made to Duke University Press for permission to
reprint excerpts from "Venus in Two Acts" by Saidiya Hartman from *Small Axe:
A Caribbean Journal of Criticism*, vol. 12, no. 2 (26), pp. 1–14, copyright © 2008
by Small Axe, Inc. All rights reserved. Republished by permission of the
copyright holder and the Publisher. www.dukepress.edu.

Library of Congress Cataloging-in-Publication Data
Names: powell, m. mick author
Title: Dead girl cameo / by m. mick powell.
Other titles: Dead girl cameo (Compilation)
Description: First edition | New York, NY: One World, [2025]
Identifiers: LCCN 2025008055 (print) | LCCN 2025008056 (ebook) |
ISBN 9780593733998 trade paperback | ISBN 9780593734001 ebook
Subjects: LCSH: African American women—Poetry | Women—Abuse of—Poetry |
Artists—Poetry | Celebrities—Death—Poetry | LCGFT: Biographical poetry
Classification: LCC PS3616.O87977 D43 2025 (print) | LCC PS3616.O87977
(ebook) | DDC 811/.6—dc23/eng/20250404
LC record available at https://lccn.loc.gov/2025008055
LC ebook record available at https://lccn.loc.gov/2025008056

Printed in the United States of America on acid-free paper

9 8 7 6 5 4 3 2 1

BOOK TEAM: Production editor: Robert Siek • Managing editor: Rebecca Berlant •
Production manager: Sarah Feightner • Copy editor: Liz Carbonell •
Proofreaders: Pam Rehm, JoAnna Kremer, and Kevin Clift

Book design by Debbie Glasserman

The authorized representative in the EU for product safety and
compliance is Penguin Random House Ireland,
Morrison Chambers, 32 Nassau Street, Dublin D02 YH68, Ireland.
https://eu-contact.penguin.ie

for Dominique,

for KJ,

for the girls we once were

Why revisit the event or the nonevent of a girl's death? . . .

How does one rewrite the chronicle of a death foretold and anticipated, as a collective biography of dead subjects, as a counter-history of the human, as the practice of freedom?

How does one listen for the groans and cries, the undecipherable songs, the crackle of fire in the cane fields, the laments for the dead, and the shouts of victory, and then assign words to all of it?

—SAIDIYA HARTMAN, "Venus in Two Acts"

CONTENTS

DEAD GIRL CAMEO

It is an impossible writing which attempts to say that which resists being said (since dead girls are unable to speak).

—SAIDIYA HARTMAN, "Venus in Two Acts"

Impossible as it is, I wanted to resurrect the girl. I wanted to retell her story as a beautiful libretto, a decadent lullaby. Making an incantation of her name, I wanted to bring her back, glorious and glittering.

I could only make from my love, from my grief, this impossible constellation—the Black Venus superstar and her spectacularized death, surrounded by media and mythology, and yet, almost as ordinary as moonrise.

I write from the planet of the unaccounted widow, to mourn my own dead loves and lovers. I reach for them here. I sing for them here. I tend to the memory of their names.

This book is written in loving and everlasting memory of:

my loves,

Kimberly "KJ" Morris   (JANUARY 19, 1979–JUNE 12, 2016)
C.L. Dominique Courts   (JANUARY 11, 1992–OCTOBER 11, 2022)

and

Billie Holiday   (APRIL 7, 1915–JULY 17, 1959)
Tammi Terrell   (APRIL 29, 1945–MARCH 16, 1970)
Minnie Riperton   (NOVEMBER 8, 1947–JULY 12, 1979)
Selena Quintanilla-Pérez   (APRIL 16, 1971–MARCH 31, 1995)
Phyllis Hyman   (JULY 6, 1949–JUNE 30, 1995)
Aaliyah Haughton   (JANUARY 16, 1979–AUGUST 25, 2001)
Lisa "Left Eye" Lopes   (MAY 27, 1971–APRIL 25, 2002)
Whitney Elizabeth Houston   (AUGUST 9, 1963–FEBRUARY 11, 2012)
Bobbi Kristina Houston Brown   (MARCH 4, 1993–JULY 26, 2015)

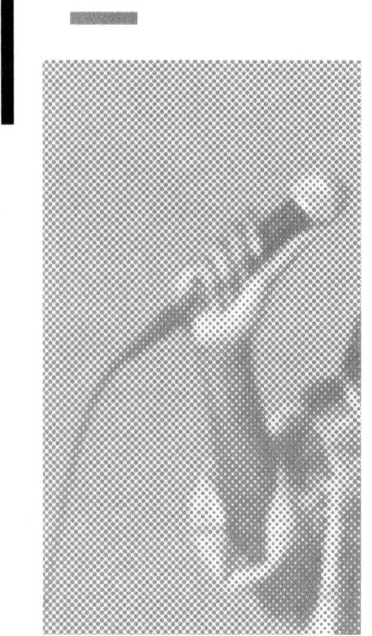

ACT I:
CHRONICLE OF A DEATH FORETOLD

*What are the kinds of stories to be told by those
and about those who live in such an intimate
relationship with death? Romances? Tragedies?
Shrieks that find their way into speech and song?*

—SAIDIYA HARTMAN, "Venus in Two Acts"

a gospel of dead girls
is called a *constellation*

annotation: girl

abjectly abracadabra: ancient anarchy babied cerulean cruel: candid camera: cool crush: desperate daughter dancing dutifully dead: daughter dancing daintily: erotically even: fuckedup frenchkiss: feigned fantastical: gang gowned ghastly: gagged godly: ghostly: hired homewrecker: heaven hurling *helpme hurtme haveme* hung in iridescent indigo: jezebel jazz joke: juke joint: jubilant kill: kaleidoscopic kindred: knockoff kink: liar liar lyre: lesbian: liminal lyric: *make me:* missus missionary: mothered manic: needed needle: nice niche: novice orgasm: organic obedience: objectified pussy plated perfectly: purple pussy palace: platinum pussy plague: quintessential rage: radiant roadkill: rattlesnake still: stillborn silent: sorrow song: taunted tortured taken tasted tainted to tar: unsung unmatched underappreciated unrequited vanity vagrancy vacancy vexing windowsill with winter wuthering waning wanting wishing whining wasting xanax *you* yellow yardbird *you* yellowing yearn *you* youthfully yielding yesteryear's zodiac

dead girl interview

What gave you your girlhood? What took it away?

Where was your mother?

What do you see when I say "scarlet"?

Do you believe in the stars?

Are there other ways you wish you died?

Can you tell me again, about the dream?

And the morning after, when the moon set?

Tell me about your closest encounter.

When did you meet her?

She is the first person you thought of—how tenderly did you touch?

What world did you invent to survive?

What world did you invent to satiate?

Tell me about your own curious rage.

Finish the sentence: "in my archive of desire, I keep _____."

What color is the thing that haunts you most?

Would you let me hold the memory?

[our mothers said:]

girl,   *you better watch yourself!*

I want you to learn some things
before you leave—

it's only the beginning

you grow in stages

there's always a price to pay
for everything

never idolize anyone

fate happens and destiny
is what you choose for yourself

Billie Holiday, from the smoking room

> *You can be up to your boobies in white satin, with gardenias in*
> *your hair and no sugar cane for miles, but you can still be working*
> *on a plantation.*

—BILLIE HOLIDAY, *Lady Sings the Blues* (1956)

It was criminal: the way I wanted and therefore
begged to be a girl, jazz-licked by a city-summer,

broken in by overuse, by overture, by how
I kissed the needle point clean of my blood.

I was supposed to be a child, once, I'm certain,
unburdened by the relentless threat of night,

dawn spawned open with a sprawling sense of rot.
Of course, I was supposed to be other things, too:

sarsaparilla, a solo flute, fae with gossamer wings,
an orchestra of machinery, something other than some

nation's redemptive flame, a country's lost chance
at growing a Black girl loved good. Despite this,

I wore my name like a long pink mink. I burned
and shunned all their ruby crowns from my head;

but there's not a girl who can say she's survived this,
no—not until the very moment she's dead.

Singer Billie Holiday Dies
Broke And Broken At 44

Billie Holiday, Queen
Of the Blues, Is Dead

Billie Holiday Writes Her Own Epitaph

"There isn't a soul on this earth who can say for sure that their fight with dope is over until they're dead."

But in the end, of course, she departed alone, her brown liveliness still an echo against the whiteness of her hospital pillow.

1959

Tammi Terrell, from the backlit bardo

Well, if Tammi Terrell is dead, you girls are looking at a ghost.

—TAMMI TERRELL, "THE ORDEAL OF TAMMI TERRELL," *Ebony* (1969)

As a girl, I was gang raped and I guess
I don't know why, but
a Black girl dressed in lilac, roped hair,
my magenta MaryJanes made
want a fate worse than whipping.

tetherlight, glixia, ribsilk
kaleidoscopekin. I do not want
the memory's lingering incense
ghosting over me.   Dancing,
to promenade; I suppose I dreamed
to balance my back in curvature,
over a stage englimmered with shadow.

that there is no shade of red in our language
proves she has always been
that which must never be crossed.
I never fixed my tongue against any mother
or the dead men they killed with nightshade,
hot ash, the whetted hilt of a gun,
their fat hearts stunted in bowls of spit,
wastes of men who wrought and wrangled
for access to a belligerent god's toolshed,
a sugardark hammer to amble a girl's neck
my mother was a girl, once, too—
pretty enough not to beg or to want

I wanted to become her shadow,

there's nowhere else to begin, but here:
why must you insist upon the starflower,
the spectacle? Yes, as a girl,
want a ceremonious gaffle,
I invented other words for gold:

shimmerah, opalmelt, sugardark.
to be martyred, to be made
anamnesis, one light forever flickering,
that's all I ever wanted; a body
of impermanence, an eternal cataclysm,
a corporeal arch over the world,
My liminal and infinite grace—

to adequately describe my mother's rage
a boundary,   a border,
I invented other words for apostasy and
never spoke a single one of their sins
their husbands with hands like sheet rock,
men's mouths slackening in a rim of light,
their funerals where mothers widowed
and whittled their bodies for circus show,
all the tetherlight absent from their skin,
see, my mother was a girl, once, too—
her mouth a scarlet peach
for no man to taste or to take

and so her shadow I became

Last Goodbye For Tammi

Pop Singer Tammi Terrell
Motown Star, Dead at 24

Singer Mourned

Last Goodbyes Said For
Tragic Tammi Terrell

The body of the 24-year-old singer, attired in a pale pink shroud, rested in a gold and bronze casket near the altar

1970

Minnie Riperton, straight from the lion's mouth

It was pretty frightening, but I wasn't afraid.

—MINNIE RIPERTON, *Sammy & Company* interview, December 13, 1975

Afraid not of the beast's ghastly jaw, I imagined
I angled its ivory fang to my artery and kept my cool
by wanting it a little more than I should have—it:

a death more instant than the bloodless drawl and
wither and whether I ever whistled again becoming
inconsequential (so says the science of vinyl

and sound-save), yes, here, the lion, its exquisite incisor,
a promise of something less sickly, assembled shock, an end
befitting a siren of the stage, unsung by the cat's cradling,

caught on camera, betrayed by a more spectacular biology.

Later in bed, I begged for it harder, even with my skull palmed
to the headstone, my throat lassoed and brining. I wanted
my bottom lip split open, wound marks left on the soft
parts of my thighs. If I could, I'd want to die on the inside
of something; I'd want to die as it swallowed me whole.

Singer-songwriter Minnie Riperton, known for the baby's breath she wore in her hair and her 1974 hit "Loving You," died of cancer here today. She was 31.

"When I perform my songs, they say a lot of things I want people to understand. I get very involved in them. Sometimes I forget how old I am. I feel mischievous, like I did in high school spitting soda through a straw at someone."

Dies At 31

Peace & Happiness Filled Minnie Riperton's Life

Minnie Riperton, 31, Sang, Wrote 'Loving You'

1979

dead girl cento

beautiful epic   come alive   fresher flowers   same lion   different part

     picture this: tropical setting   cockatoo on the arm   I strike the pose again

however it was   however it happened   however it finished

     the bird was gone   but the bird   did something   yesterday

Hers is the same fate as every other Black Venus.

—SAIDIYA HARTMAN, "Venus in Two Acts"

alternate ending, ending in song

You should know it was a curfewed quiet: my father the room
over, pulling steam from a Pall Mall, my mother staged starry
somewhere South, begging, in her own self-righteous way;

my two brothers, rambunctious with their youth, and me, girl-
child with an early fixation for coppered candy, rope of metal.
If I let myself think about it, the evening was ordinary enough:

a plate of rice for dinner, dry cereal for dessert, playing outside
my parents' bedroom in my paisley-printed dress. It was an odd old
comfort, running the smooth tip of the wire hanger over my tongue,

cool tool skating circles in my mouth. How I drooled all over
that sweet hanger, even when paint began to peel off its steel.
Still, I can't remember which brother wrestled me down, only

the hook hurling itself to the back of my throat, its excruciating entry.
Instinctually, I yanked the wire back up, slashed a slit centimeters
from my vocal cords, my mouth babbling with an undrinkable blood.

My father filled my wound with tissues, caressed and cooed whenever
we ran a red light. In the emergency room, a surgeon sutured my split
roof, stuck his instruments past my tonsils and knit me a new throat.

I mourn my false memory of the monstrous girl-child
who stood up during her surgery, clamped her maw
around the doctor's fists, and drew a newfangled crimson.

She set him free only to unstitch the corset from her mouth—
to preserve that private wreckage early on, long before
the callous world taught her how to wear her singular name.

If I were to be completely honest with you, I would say
I still see her sometimes, dancing in the smoke, lounging

on the zebra-striped love seat, smizing over a bourbon
in her hospital gown. Sometimes I see her in the studio, across

the stage, older now but still a girl, in the Kamali suit, a violet hole
constantly widening in her throat. She wears her hair like I'd like to,

curved short just below the ear. She thirsts for yogurts, caviar, rose mint
tea, easy things to swallow. She lives to make a spectacle of my ruin,

and I would have to say it's her laugh that enchants me most, how she throws
her pulse back and the sound comes from the open cuts behind her teeth.

So yes, I suppose the world almost missed out on Whitney,
or maybe Whitney Elizabeth Houston almost missed out on the world,

who's to say?

All I know is when I see her, I'm certain there's a Heaven
somewhere, someplace, where it didn't have to end this way.

[I was looking for my young womanhood,]
even when I was a little girl.

I had been given this gift,
the gift of song.

I open my mouth and there it is.

I   open

    my   mouth

and   there   I   open

    my   mouth

        and   there

it   is.   I   open

    my   mouth

and   there   I   open

    my mouth

      and   there

        it   is.

annotation: Phyllis Hyman performs "You Know How to Love Me" on *Dinah!* (1979)

> PAUL WILLIAMS: The next guest is someone Clive Davis should introduce because she's one of Arista's great rising stars; she's a singer that's already been compared to Billie Holiday, is that not true, Clive?
>
> CLIVE DAVIS: She has; she's a triple-threat star and equally as powerful in every category, whether that's jazz, rhythm and blues, pop—great singing, and an incredible-looking woman as well. I'll just introduce her by saying America's biggest new star will be Ms. Phyllis Hyman.
>
> —PAUL WILLIAMS AND CLIVE DAVIS, *Dinah!* interview, 1979

in her gilded skirt set, Phyllis croons,
      ganders at love like a perfect gown
            set at a price too steep. her girl-self
                  would not let her dream the kind of dreams
            other girls dreamed, and perhaps all eldest
      daughters are cursed to make worship songs
for the stifled god of their desires—

with her subtle cinematics, control of contralto,
      Phyllis spins the spell like a wanted premonition.
      her bridled desire, its unending percussion,
a languid lyric pleading like a phantom's refrain:

            is your heart at the center?
            is this just a different kind of pain?

INTERVIEWER: How would you describe yourself as a woman trying to deal with life in the '80s?

PHYLLIS HYMAN: Well, I don't deal with it very well . . . I'm born under the sign of Cancer, and I have a Sagittarian moon and rising, and if you know anything about the signs, that's called extreme highs and extreme lows; there is no middle for me.

—Ebony/Jet Showcase interview, 1987

**annotation: Whitney Houston performs "Home"
on *The Merv Griffin Show* (1983)**

> MERV GRIFFIN: Today [Clive Davis] has brought his latest discovery with him and she is, in two words, simply breathtaking.

> CLIVE DAVIS: If the mantle is to pass to someone who is nineteen, who is elegant, who is sensuous, who is innocent, who's got an incredible range of talent but guts and soul at the same time, it would be Whitney Houston.

in her very first televised performance,
Whitney Houston wears a royal violet blouse,
a straight-hemmed skirt, her baby hairs wisped
across her forehead, two gold rings.

the stage is decorated with stars, with light, nearly lilac.
the audience, almost instantly, is stunned to silence.

here, she prophesizes her plight, her nascent yearn
for a fictive home, imploring *time to slow up,*
to give her time to grow up.

Cissy Houston, her mother, strikes the band
from behind the iridescent stage curtains,
her shadow orchestrating a gorgeous surmise,
the music matched perfectly to Whitney's momentum,
her certitude, her unwieldy and God-given power.

Robyn Crawford, her love, watches from home,
marvels at the way Whitney sparkles, how
she made it all seem easy, natural. no strain at all.

Whitney wields every note like a delicacy,
her mouth anchored around a loud syllable,
a breathless vibrato, her cheeks blushed
in their last girlish pink, her slender arms
framing her face, opening her chest,
her hands most desperate and reaching

Phyllis tells Whitney the truth

Girl, you've gotta know they want you dead!
  They'll kill your Black ass without blinking!

They'll mine your voice for whatever the price!
  They'll slice your throat while you're singing!

Girl, I've watched these men conspire,
  I've seen them lace their tongues with Satan's!

In rooms wall to wall with *our* earned gold,
  I've watched them take glory for our bacon!

Girl, we've got to keep the music in our hearts;
  we've got to make our own kind of song!

And Baby, I know it's easy to get weary—
  we've got to work at this our whole life long!

So you just keep calling on me when it gets real hard;
  call on me when your heart gets real real heavy.

Call on me when you want to hurt them back—
  call on me; you know I'll be ready.

Picture them: The relics of two girls, one cradling the other, plundered innocents; a sailor caught sight of them and later said they were friends.

—SAIDIYA HARTMAN, "Venus in Two Acts"

IN THAT OTHER FANTASY WHERE WE LIVE FOREVER

We each wrote a page about our love, pledged that we would
always be honest and loyal, and left our past there. We signed it
on February 13, 1982. . . . It would be our secret, and it would
hold us together.

—ROBYN CRAWFORD, *A Song for You: My Life with Whitney Houston*

I made, of my bones, an earth for you: turned the oceans
your favorite shade of light, that deepened, nearly bruised
dusk. Reflected in my palms, what I've made into water
glows amethyst; when you drink from it, you are iridescent,
luminous, lilting. I am metallic, meticulous in the way
I pronounce your full name, watch you watch the world.
I have quieted galaxies for this moment, hushed the moral pleading,
called the caged animal in from the ark. *Today, tomorrow, world with-*
out an end; to love you much and yet to love you more, to want
to hold your body to mine as midnight settles in the jasmine trees.
And, by light of our stars, make water for tea gathered from the garden,
read from Giovanni in the living room, dance to Hathaway in the hall;
lie with our legs laced together in our bedclothes and watch,
quietly, knowingly, for our moon's sweeping, predictable fall.

last love song for Nippy

*In preparation for the trip, Nip and I looked at her itinerary and
laid out clothing for each performance, meet and greet, dinner, and
interview. . . . We assembled outfits with accessories and Whitney
tried on each combination and did a fashion show for me. . . .*

This was [Nip's] first voyage on the supersonic jet. . . .

Whitney Elizabeth Houston was taking off, full speed ahead.

—ROBYN CRAWFORD, A Song for You: My Life with Whitney Houston

after a warm bath with citrus soaps, you lean against the ledge naked, lather your legs.
I lay the face of the razor at the base of your ankle and begin to trace upwards, past your
knee. you lacquer your skin with baby oil, press your nose to the glass plate once more,
wait for the ache to subside. tomorrow. tomorrow will return the good of your girlhood to
its resting place: that East Orange basketball court, that pulpit, that passenger's seat, the
inner seam of your mother's church dress, your hair hugged to the nape of your neck. *Nip
in the knee-length shorts. Nip in the Adidas Gazelles, galloping.* Nip, tomorrow you will
be a girl on a jet plane, your singular name whipped out into stars. tonight we take hot iron
to glittering fabric and to the wilding strands of your hair, to the backs of our wrists with
love. tonight you insist on cigarettes, catwalk, dancing to Donny Hathaway half-dressed,
your bare heart touched to mine, your soft, slow grind. tonight you insist I
kiss you for the last time and cut your collarbone in the right light. you, all peach skin
and desperate and alive electrically, untouched, coke-charged and moon-bright. *Nip, of all the
songs you ever sang, of all the songs you'll ever sing.* Nip, I never said I was afraid of how
long we would love; I only feared how little we'd forget.

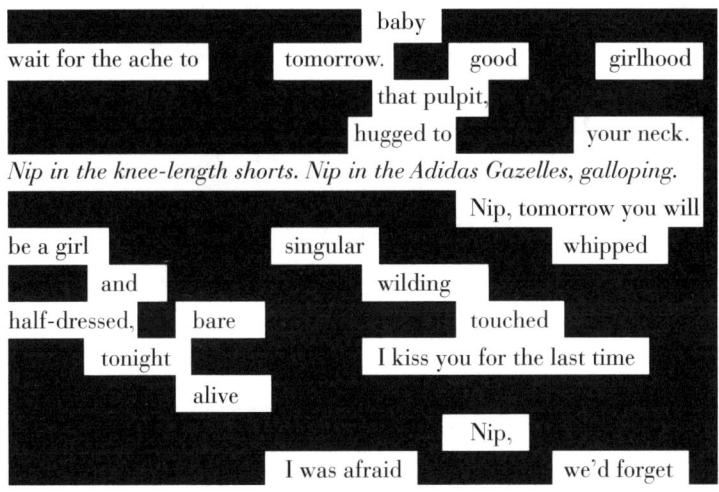

baby, tomorrow

you will be a girl   whipped   bare

I kiss you   alive

All expectations met by Whitney Houston

Pop: Whitney Houston In Carnegie Hall Debut

Sensuous Whitney Houston Is Sizzling With Success With "You Give Good Love"

Singer Whitney Houston Gives A Riveting, Classy Performance

Whitney Houston's Success Is Global
Rising Star Enjoying Simultaneous Hits in U.S., Europe

Whitney Houston charms fans with lyrical pathos

I know enough about moderation

It's no wonder to me that Whitney's first single to top
the charts was the one where she's waiting; a reservoir
drenched in silk, narcissus, amber, violet, vetiver.

Released four days after her twenty-second birthday,
"Saving All My Love for You" makes her a woman,
wanting and wander-lusting. I wait while Whitney

wails onstage or rolls from the Rolls-Royce into a pink
penthouse suite. I wait in our bedroom while she busies
her cherried mouth, making heartache a hexagonal thing.

I know that I am animal by the way I lick her back,
her breasts pressed against the hardwood, a memory
I recount again (again) at dusk. In the kitchen, I break

into the belly of a fish, rinse it clean of its guts over the sink.
I want to fill it with something;   her womb aches
every third week of the month, conjures an uninhabitable hunger.

The seabass shimmers dead on the countertop, my hands
prepared to cleave. She makes an art of acquiescence:
the knife grasping light beside the fish. The fish, once

grappling for air, submerged in oxygen. Between us, this
unquenchable, ceaseless negotiation—in my dreams,
I know enough about moderation to leave before we burn

the house down. It is too easy not to tell her how often
I want her to make green the thing that lost its gold,
to purple the thrust of my throat. Too easy to admit

how little we know of our own villainy, how little we know
of this cannibalistic desire or the heart that never tires of its list.
What is it about this love that kills the good animal in each of us?

What is it about this love that makes me forget I am free?

SUBLIMATION

there are still impossible requests
I wish to make of your body—
its gemstones' metallic kiss,
your spine spun into its begging arch.
there are dreams in which
my fingers tangle into your hair,

dreams in which I follow you
directly into the ominous spill

I write my night away to forge
an inconceivable amnesia,
to breach the subtle difference
between *stifle* and *suffocate*,
control and *relinquish*,
desire and the deading of that desire

as impossible as it is to kill.

here I should tell you how
I've come by my own hand
and quietly convinced myself
it was yours, as quietly as
I've confessed to the depth
of my heart's unending song,
its pleading metronome,
its languid, beating trill.

the morning after [oh venus in taurus night]

by the bladed sun of daybreak, I slip
into myself, tingle from ankle to tip
as if touched by you. you, habitual
imaginary, sophic with all the ways   I open
                                              I open   my legs to the smell
                                              of clover, sweetwater, vanilla musk.
                                              my hands play your palm: how tender
                                              I tend to the memory of your entering.

                                              to enter,   you might have slicked
                                                          two fingers in the basin
                                                          between your teeth.
                                                          negotiated the pulse.
                                                          snuffed out the amber
                                                          candle to find my spot.

to find my spot, you'd
press your thumb
into the well of my throat
and wait for a whimper—
a whimper desperate green,
a phantasmagoric plead
pled to the hook. remember,
Darling, how you'd make me
trill? how I'd quaver, come canary
in the nightclub stall, Pontiac backseat,

the motel's secret sacred tomb?   we were supposed to be

quiet   then
quiet   as a familiar chorus

                                              but should I tell them, my Love,
                                              of the song I would sing?

                                              how I swept up your name
                                              into every breathless lyric?

RESIGNATION

Stung with pine clove, we were nearly trees, we were nearly girls
with twin crescent moons scorned at our throats; this too, I'm sure,

a zodiac for girls called *ladies* as girls and often called *marvelous*
but never marveled *at:* beautiful only in hindsight, though this still

made us vain, vanity being our mothers' third tongue.
Don't you remember synching our sullied blood and why

and how and when a Black girl becomes a sapling, she becomes
an encyclopedia of boom, brake, and sully, silly bug with black

lace panties put around her ankles, crown of sugar-wasted bees
waltzing about her braids or be she crowned silly sullied girl

wasted with lace and breaking the moist ache from her panties over
the bathroom sink—can you smell it still? Don't you remember

the motel room, Motown grind all neck and hip, hand-holding to tears,
dancing to an Aretha anthem while we waited, your spine bent to mine,

my hand, at once, on the back of your neck? My gorgeous, my guardian,
godmother to our Beloved, how could you not know? And of course I still do.

You are my best, you are my only, you are my storybook love,
but Love, I've already said it was beautiful—it was beautiful,

yes, and it was full of heartache.

If it is not possible to undo the violence that inaugurates the sparse record of a girl's life or remedy her anonymity with a name or translate the commodity's speech, then to what end does one tell such stories? How and why does one write a history of violence?

—SAIDIYA HARTMAN, "Venus in Two Acts"

**annotation: ten-year-old Aaliyah performs
"My Funny Valentine" on *Star Search* (1989)**

if Baby Girl ever was,   then she sprung from this stage

    with permission to envision a valentine her age:

*a pink cardstock card hand-painted
on the thirteenth day, given to the girl
best friend who was loved and loved
differently in a winter that made song
a tangible instrument*

       or

*two cherried children twirling
their fingers to each other's
wrists and running towards
a top-loose hydrant, the cool water
star-silver and shouting*

is not so gd to be born a girl

In a 2001 interview with *Vibe* magazine, Aaliyah shared, "My mother always said that she feels like I always had sex appeal. Even when I was very young, when I would take pictures, there was something sexual about me." She repeated various iterations of this statement throughout her career, which formally began at fifteen years old when she released her first album, *Age Ain't Nothin But A Number* (*AANBAN*, 1994). *AANBAN* was written and produced by defamed superstar and notorious, convicted sexual abuser R. Kelly "[e]specially for Aaliyah," as noted on the album's promos and back cover. In its writing, Kelly uses the narrative voice of a teenage girl to detail her friendships, communities, and sexuality.

The album's eponymous song opens with Aaliyah's voiceover: "May fifth, 1993, Aaliyah's diary."

On this date, in real time, Aaliyah was fourteen years old.

Kathy Iandoli identifies Aaliyah as "R. Kelly's Lost Survivor" in her 2021 biography, *Baby Girl: Better Known as Aaliyah*, because Aaliyah's experiences are often excluded from conversations surrounding Kelly's egregious patterns of sexual predation and violent, grotesque abuse of young Black girls and women. At twenty-seven years old, rising singer-songwriter R. Kelly used his star-power to bribe a city clerk into falsifying Aaliyah's age on identification documents so the two could get married. In *Baby Girl*, Iandoli gives the details of the nondisclosure agreement signed by Aaliyah, her parents, and Kelly less than a month after the date on their marriage certificate:

> [O]n September 29, 1994 . . . [the signed] agreement states that R. Kelly is to pay $100 [allegedly a cover for $3 million] to Aaliyah in exchange for cutting ties altogether and never

mentioning their relationship again "due to the nature of the music industry and its ability to engender rumors and disseminate personal information, both true and untrue." . . . Further, R. Kelly was not held accountable for anything that happened, or anything that may happen, even "a decline in her ability, reputation, or marketability . . . emotional distress caused by any aspect of her business or personal relationship with Robert . . . [or] physical injury or emotional pain and suffering from any assault or battery perpetrated by Robert against her person."

On September 29, 1994, Aaliyah was fifteen years old.

Six months later, at the 1995 Soul Train Music Awards, Aaliyah was booed when she announced the nominations for Best R&B/Soul or Rap New Artist and when *AANBAN* was nominated for Best R&B/Soul Album. This is a mortifying experience she shares with Whitney Houston, who was booed at the 1989 Soul Train Music Awards while other audience members yelled out "White-y, White-y," a criticism claiming that Whitney was a sellout and not Black enough. For Aaliyah, the audience's jeering seemed to be in response to Aaliyah's professional and public separation from R. Kelly, a cruelty stemmed from the cultural repulsion at a survivor's survival. At the 1995 Soul Train Music Awards, R. Kelly won Best R&B/Soul Single for "Bump n' Grind."

Aaliyah was sixteen years old.

INTERVIEWER: Is there something you regret today that you've done?

AALIYAH: Regret? Regret what? There's nothing to regret. It was a hard time for me, so, I mean, you know, I learned you've got to be strong . . . you just have to have strength. . . . It's even in my family to survive . . . it's in my blood to be a survivor.

—*P3 Soul* interview, 1996

Aaliyah's Spirit Sounds Like a 'Million'

★★★½   ★★★½   ★★★½

teen bride   teen bride

pretty appendage.   pretty appendage.

irresistible version   irresistible version

girl with admitted

poise and precocity—
girl with admitted   the most convincing
                                              marvel
poise and precocity—
the most convincing
marvel   Aaliyah

Aaliyah   teasingly witchy

Aaliyah
                                              young
all of this
                              on the money.

ARSENIO HALL: A lot of critics write about you all being feminist rappers—what do you think about that?

LISA "LEFT EYE" LOPES: I'm the rapper, okay? Now, you can call me a feminist rapper if you want to—I'm not one, but . . .

—TLC on The Arsenio Hall Show, 1992

Left Eye backstage with her whole hand in her mouth

& I take it in like a wonder / this velvet thing / this knuckled crystal / this supernova of viole(n)t sensation / a soft descent into the scent of tobacco oud / & somewhere / *yes* / I am still a girl / with an easy jaw / full feasted / & someone threads beads at the end of my braids / & backstage / the beads make a ballad with the bass / & the bass becomes the mouth of the field / & I am dancing with the dead / on the dandelion dance floor / the phantoms / illuminate it into a bardo / & bleed fluorescent all around me / they paint the surrounding space / with their electric homicide / *yes* / the fist still a statue between my teeth / & this is not part of the end / our ancient & implied sensuality / two celestial bodies bursting / into one another at once / a stellar collision / & we know now / that a stellar collision gave us gold / & so I turn to the phantoms / & so I say to the phantoms / that I am not interested in anything / that doesn't produce gold / & in this blossoming field / this cemetery for girls / I am plasma wet & only emerging / & they marvel at it— / the miraculous unpretty / the gargantuan mouth

[in a fiery surrender]

Lisa surrendered—

        set fire to the story
        belonging to her boyfriend
        Lopes, destroyed in the Thursday blaze

        her right, her habit
        her misdemeanor
        found in the burned-out rage

        Lopes set fire
        to a mansion
        after Rison slapped her

        before any beautiful troubles,
        a firing handgun

[the house of evil burned]

Yes, he kissed my hand.
He was romantic, told me:
"I've waited for you."

I had no freedom.
Could not recognize myself.
Nobody heard me.

How did I do it?
I burned what I kept inside.
You want to know how?

My lighter fluid.
Bathtub full of tennis shoes.
My face bruised, broken.

I was the victim;
got hypnotized by the flames.
I was the victim.

Yeah, motherfucker.
You can't believe anything.
That's the gospel truth.

Left Eye cackling in front of the flame

what else to call this thing besides bestial
hunger or brutal thirst?   my mouthsnarl
englimmered with sparkle, a new dress
ballooned out of cloudsmoke.   here is where I danced
into the denim sea,   drank gasoline straight from my hands.
here is where I watched
a woman hold   a needle steady until it disappeared
into her arm. until amber-empty.   until graceless moon.
until curtained window   opened to a vintage death. here:
the prettier sister. necklace of knuckle. reflection
of fire until we turned *femme&flame*,   kissed with the cruelty
of a castle built in a world   without fairytale,
the most ordinary of burnings.
while men named after planets or sculptors   gawked from bell towers
in Basquiat crowns, I embered,   I built to an envied climax,
flame-drenched with wonder, and whispered:

> *unfurl your fist and show me*
> *a bouquet of collected canine teeth;*
> *blow blunt smoke into my mouth*
> *and call me lover girl four times fast.*
> *tell your skeleton to pop posies and ornament*
> *in loose gold. tell me I'm pretty.*
> *tell me you're about to come.*

hostage

After the release of TLC's 1994 sophomore album, *CrazySexy-Cool*, Left Eye, T-Boz, Chilli, and a group of women Lisa met during her forced detention at the diversion center stormed into Arista Records armed with guns, looking for Clive Davis.

While the album had generated over $75 million for the multibillion-dollar record company, TLC's cut collectively totaled $150,000. Left Eye, T-Boz, and Chilli wanted their fair share of the profit they had worked for, nearly died for.

Recounting the story on *The Mo'Nique Show* in 2009, T-Boz said, "Of course Lisa was the ringleader."

PHYLLIS HYMAN: Clive Davis taught me to never be afraid because I was so terrorized by him. Whether he meant to do it or not I'll never know. But he sure taught me that if you try to terrorize me again—well, we can't say that on public radio, what I may do to someone who tries to hurt me again in this business. I'm not having it. I should be respected as I respect, and I will not have someone try to ruin my spirit and ruin my career.

If Clive Davis . . . if his plan was to destroy my career, it didn't work.

—*P3 Soul* interview, 1994

Phyllis Hyman refused to be lonely

I REFUSE TO BE LONELY

I REFUSE TO REVERSE MY TONGUE

I REFUSE THE REFUSAL OF MY RIGHTS

I REFUSE THE REFUSAL OF MY SEX

I REFUSE TO BE LONELY

I REFUSE TO BE LAUGHED AT

I REFUSE THE THEFT OF BLACK LABOR

I REFUSE TO COME UNDERDRESSED

I REFUSE TO BE LESS LOUD

I REFUSE TO BE LESS BLACK

I REFUSE TO BE LONELY

I REFUSE TO ABSORB THIS CURIOUS RAGE

I REFUSE TO ABSORB THIS CURIOUS RAGE

I REFUSE TO ABSORB THIS CURIOUS RAGE

I REFUSE YOU MY SONG

I REFUSE YOU MY NAME

I REFUSE YOU MY VOICE

I REFUSE TO BE BLAMED

I REFUSE YOU MY HEART

I REFUSE YOU MY LIFE

I REFUSE YOU MY BEAUTY

I REFUSE YOUR SHARP KNIFE

Singer Phyllis Hyman dead at 45

The tragic death of Phyllis Hyman
Authorities say R&B singer may have committed suicide

A death foretold
Phyllis Hyman's final album served as a poignant suicide note

———

1995

dead girl pastoral

it is too easy to turn to the doe
dead in the meridian, looking
for a labyrinth like a metaphor;

too easy to say the grass that grew
to a shroud was sweetgrass, rhizomic
and made golden by a baneful sun;

it is easy to make, of her bronze neck,
an oak branch broke by lightning,
splintered where the muscle strains to sing;

and easier to name her blood a body
of water, a salt marsh or shoal, crimson
spill weaving out into the street.

it is an impossibility to pronounce her dead
to her herd of deer who watch and wait,
who wallow in the womb of a forested grief.

Two world-less girls found a country in each other's
arms. Beside the defeat and the terror, there
would be this too: the glimpse of beauty,
the instant of possibility.

—SAIDIYA HARTMAN, "Venus in Two Acts"

You let me kiss you in the nightclub.
In Johannesburg. In Asbury Park. In Orlando. In your curt-cut sequined skirt. On the pulsing purple dance floor. In the sweltering bathroom stall. Through blades of rain. When the streetlights hushed. You let me kiss you. On the mouth. On your neck. Up your arm. Against the cool brick. To the dyke DJ's disco track. You let me kiss you. With my hands in your hair. At the first lesbian bachelorette party. When your song spun the walls. Before last call. Before the cops kicked down the doors. Until you became violet. You let me kiss you. As the drag queen strung us up with her pearl boa. In your emerald suit. Onstage, once. You let me kiss you. After you begged for it. After you pleaded. After a line of coke. After we saw two other girls tethered at the lips, one girl's thigh between the other's hips, their sweet, slow grind a mirror to your want. You let me kiss you. In the smoky alleyway. In the Pontiac. In the place you felt most free. The place you felt most invisible. You let me kiss you. Copper-dark. Hard. Hauntingly. I wanted you. To kiss me back.

REPORTER: One thing that haunts Whitney is the many questions about her love life. Whitney has repeatedly denied any rumors that she is gay.

WHITNEY HOUSTON: I don't make it a habit of putting out in the street whom I'm sleeping with. . . . I think it's because [the public doesn't] know, because I do keep my life to myself. . . . I've come from being a lesbian to a whore.

—Inside Edition interview, 1991

gender is holographic

why cut the silhouette / shadow sharp in the dressing room / why hide the frame / why reach for one's own reflection / while the object of desire burns / why her fingers fisting into / a nebulous wet / a Whitney in white / suited for dyke bar / why the throwback / to Dietrich dancing the line / her arrogant swagger across the club / suggestive stare / between the blonde / and the blue light / every hand gloved in ivory / belongs to a femme here / gender is holographic / hallucinated / take this hand / against her wrist / take these versions of herself / supreme femme to infinity / five funhouse mirrors / singing the shadow to form / still / softened jaw / something unsaid / face lit by black / the fact that it could be anyone / proves that it could be anyone / dancing the line / Whitney whips a bike / tilts a sapphic smile / towards a setting moon

annotation: Whitney Houston performs "Heartbreak Hotel" live at the MTV 13th Annual New York City Lesbian and Gay Pride Dance (1999)

> *It was a perfect warm, hazy June night, and the pier was packed with more than seven thousand. . . . Whit vibed off the crowd as though they'd lifted her off the ground, jumping up and down joyfully, never showing the slightest sign of fatigue. I'd never seen her like that.*

> —ROBYN CRAWFORD, *A Song for You: My Life with Whitney Houston*

at the last ball of the century, Whitney wears capris.
without falter or fatigue, her stage emits an intimacy
akin to a private bedroom joyful dance. she jumps and
gestures to an audience jubilant at the mere fact of her
survival, her smile half-mooned in the magenta stars.

The queers queen her humanity, harmonize with her
heartbreak, her vulnerable desires cascaded out and
into the winking June skyline. almost for the first time,
Whitney finds the home she quested among a kink
of glamouring gays, a haze of chromatic smoke.

energized, she spins herself silly, Black with glee.

when Aaliyah met Kidada

Black girl of my Black girl heart / Black girl of my Black girl heart's yearning / we were figured from the same future / first edition freaks / Android enigmatic / finger waves and glazed chocolate lips / hot pink minks and leopard-print two-seaters / our extravagant leathers / velour track suits and bangled charm bracelets / our magics were meant to be intertwined / a connection predestined by the gods and the zodiacs alike / time is nothing / between soulmates / and your opulence is a fortune I am fortunate enough to indulge in / your aura / resplendent respite /

your Black girl heart

home home home

to my lonely Black girl heart

[people thought they were lesbians]

We wound up in a beautiful suburban neighborhood, and I photo-
graphed [Aaliyah and Kidada] . . . people thought they were
lesbians. . . . They were just rolling around and laughing and rid-
ing on each other's backs. It was fun and beautiful.

—JAYSON KEELING on photographing AALIYAH and KIDADA JONES

for *Oneworld* magazine (1997), *Autre* magazine interview (2018)

Strangers speculated a sapphic song
lilted from the girls' cherry lavender lips.

From their cherry lavender lips, they lilted,
clung tight to each other like their given names.

There are names given to girls who cling to each other.
There are girls given to names that echo their want.

Want was an echo given Baby Girl's name before
Baby Girl herself became a synonym for *gone*.

One girl, becoming herself, becomes a synonym for _____.
The other: a kind of widow, a storied silhouette.

This could've been the other kind of story: no shadow,
only her incessant lyric in the sweet spring sprawl.

In the sprawl of spring, a lyric so incessantly sweet,
strangers speculated a sapphic song.

More Than a Woman **as category of gender**

flip-switch femme

   dyke debonair

      dyke debutante

         deciduously deciphered

            lipstick lover who loves lipstick
              on another lipstick lover

                 an excess accessory

                 an exorbitant pleasure

                 secrets, treasures

                 keeps on getting better

"Rock the Boat" is a song about strapping, if for no other reason than

my own selfish association:

> femme dyke combing their room in cerulean light /
>
> Aphrodite's sage / a song played just for me /
>
> smooth synthesizer / silicone slick & slayed across
>
> their waist / thirst for synthetic champagne / sweat
>
> & strawberry for the wet / for the way / they stroked
>
> / before sliding inside / this is not a synonym / or
>
> unsubstantiated sapphic lust / it's a matter of fact /
>
> the phallic absence :   the catamaran of femmes
>
> pushing their pelvic bones together :   ocean agape
>
> & scissored against an amethyst sky, tender as the morning
>
> ushered out the moon—this lover / my love / our acrobatics
>
> suspending us / above fields of yarrow & honeysuckle /
>
> the song of their name / a sweet plea / salacious sacrament
>
> / a swell before softening / saturated / satiated / swimming
>
> & coming closer / the proverbial appetite / an incessant
>
> kaleidoscopic rain /

The promiscuity of the archive begets a wide array of reading, but none that are capable of resuscitating the girl.

—SAIDIYA HARTMAN, "Venus in Two Acts"

Akasha, Queen of the Damned, eating the beating heart

I take a generous taste of the mortal's mouth
before I snap its bones—although centuries
of stone turned my palate to ash, my body
still thrummed with the wet of a god. God,

I missed most this foreplay: appraisal of a throat,
vein, cut, and bulge, appetite fueled by the hot
touch of tongue. Yes, a queen is a creatural thing,
and the part of me who wears that garter hungers

delectable pleasures: red metal silk sweet carnage.
pickled perfect anatomy. holographic nectar malted
with the salt of mortality. But what good is an entree
without an exquisite appetizer, a violent savoring?

At the heart of the dance floor, I dissipate, dip my hips
to an electric guitar, scowl my seduction before I stake
my nails through the mortal's thymus and diaphragm,
kiss its pulsing organ to my time-sharpened teeth. Please,

have the cameraman do a close-up to catch the dripping
ruby of my fangs, to make a metaphor of this peculiar
vampiric lust thrust upon my living self. Before I die,
I need them to see me vile, my vengeance venomous

and unyielding. They must know my prophecy, its fiery
truth beheld: *you kill me, you kill yourselves.*

AALIYAH: It's dark in my favorite dream. Someone is following me. I don't know why. I'm scared. Then I suddenly take off. I fly away. Far away. How do I feel about it?

As if I were floating in the air. Free. Weightless. No one can reach me. No one can touch me. A wonderful feeling.

—*Die Zeit* interview, 2001

R&B star Aaliyah
dies in plane crash

*A tragedy after the
filming of a video in
the Bahamas.*

Aaliyah, 22, Singer Who First Hit the Charts at 14

Singer, Actress Aaliyah Dies;
R&B Albums Topped Charts

*A Diva
Without
An Attitude*

Aaliyah's Fans Mourn
Hip-Hop's Latest Loss

Singer Dies With 7 Others in Plane Crash

2001

good-bye, summer

August 25, 2001: where were you when you heard that Aaliyah died?

hot comb summer   singe of sweet straight   from the scalp   spun in leather seat

     my stylist today has hot pink nails   bejeweled   and   long that *stretchhhhhh*

beyond my brow my sweat collects beneath them   i don't look in the mirror

     my black cape   is so plastic i hate plastic   i hate velcro

around my neck   i close my eyes   my eyes are closed   *i gotta crush on you*

     & *that is true indeed*   Aaliyah is my favorite   and   i love all her songs

and she's on   and   she's on again   and   i press hard with my thigh bones

     into the chair   i press harddd harddd   i am eight   and electric

and Aaliyah is on   and   i love her harddd   and   now on the radio

     there is a man i mistake his voice for god   my eyes are closed   i am eight

and god says   that she's dead   that she died   i am eight

     and my first crush is dead   my first crush has died   i am eight

in a hair salon   i am eight   and   blkgrl   still   electric

     my stylist today has hot pink nails   and   i want to stick them into my eyes

i want   to stick them into my eyes   i hate velcro   i hate velcro around my neck

     i hate this pounding   around my neck   between my legs   Aaliyah is dead

Aaliyah is on   on again   *did i kill her?*   my mother   is crying

     my stylist is crying   my stylist   has hot pink nails   i want to

stick them   into my eyes   i want to   stick them   into my eyes   even though

     i don't   understand   quite yet   what it means   to be gone

[there's so many ways that you can die]

LISA "LEFT EYE" LOPES: [Aaliyah's death] did come as a shock, it's a pretty hard one to swallow, especially the way that she went because there's so many ways that you can die, you know, and that's a pretty tragic way to go.

I do believe that there's an afterlife. . . . I'm sure that there are people who are close to Aaliyah who will definitely feel her presence, even though she's not here in this physical realm.

a truce addressed in chemical lace / a truth: I learnt to devour by the scoured bone / by the callous scraped clean / the process itself requires a sacrificial fabric / to disintegrate into the other / and an ether as well / can be two things: incendiary / deceitful in its odor / obscure in its distance / it depends on the discipline / in astrology / to carry a sun / and Venus in the same sign / indicates you love expressively / who knows why / after Aaliyah died / I took to needle-pricking my knee / constellating Capricorn / a sarsaparilla / what a scared, scared girl / stashed in the birdbath of her own pearly throat / only we know secretly / the choker symbolizes something else / you could not imagine / two moons split by an unencumbered sky / such a wet darkness /

LAST DAYS OF LEFT EYE

When I was a kid,
I wished all of this: little
girl, gifted dreamer.

Planets and stars born,
highest number next to God,
certain chemistry—

TLC breathed life
into a beautiful song,
truly authentic.

I was overjoyed
to be in that place, happy
how we made magic.

My problems stemmed from
saying too much, creating
bad times and struggles.

I'm a Gemini.
Somebody got to be smart
enough not to break.

But, tell me, why does
it always happen to us?
The things we go through?

I would like to be
someone who removes the smoke.
The one thing I learned?

I learned how to love
myself; if I don't love me,
I can't, won't, survive.

No more chasing waterfalls

'Crazy' member of Grammy-winning R&B trio TLC killed in Honduran car crash

Lisa Lopes, Rapper, Dies in Honduras Crash at 30

Singer Died in Idyllic Setting Where She Sought New Life

2002

dead girl chorus

i understand what i cannot love most: girl dead twenty-two
    feet from the aircraft, balded by its brutal flame.

nor the girl bitten by a ghastlier beast, her forever
    eyes darkening, hidden behind a tinted frame.

start here instead: girl, red as a cardinal, in the skin-cut skirt
    of a serpent, no stiletto-sharpened shame,

or here: in her oceanic dress, Venusian kiss, crystallized
    from the future, before the fatal fame.

So it is tempting to fill in the gaps and to provide closure where there is none. To create a space for mourning where it is prohibited. To fabricate a witness to a death not much noticed.

—SAIDIYA HARTMAN, "Venus in Two Acts"

the duet of Whitney and Bobbi Kristina

I needed to love you the way I knew:
down to the bone, as an ambulance set
to drown out the screaming sirens—
tenderness, my child, is a luxury,
an extravagant ivory heirloom
we did not inherit. we bloomed
cruel gardens instead of softened
starlight, full moon harvest of
pixie dust and clutter and another
cursed addiction claimed by tabloid,
a hunger so wrought by wreckage;

how a mother loves her only daughter
to her grave: genetic propensity for fracture,
the anguish that eats and eats because
a lesson learned most easily by breaking
is a lesson well-deserved.
our womanhoods blank in rough
shame, a lonely gender formed by
cut and claw. a girl will grow into her own
mother afraid of her listless want,
twisted fuck in the smoke-shot backseat,
a thirst so hungry for respite.

AT THE MIDNIGHT OF MY LIFE

The Beverly Hilton, Room 434, Beverly Hills, CA, February 2012

In the very same room where I was taught
    how to wear my singular name,

I whipped myself with cashmere, jewel tones. Glittering
    like a hallucination,

I set the sink to stage: stung out the crystal, whiskey,
    whimsical pill cartwheeling down my throat.

•

I whipped myself, hallucinated the cashmere lined
    with jewels, the glittered tones,

while I sunk the stage to set: whiskeyed the whimsical crystal
    down and out my cartwheeled throat.

I gave myself one last circus with the circuits blaring
    in a blue-white winter, an academy of bellowing gowns.

•

I staged the set to sink: crystaled my whiskey throat and
    cartwheeled out and down down down—

one last blaring circus, an academy of short-circuits,
    a gown of winters white-blue and bellowing.

A skeletal skeptic, I surrendered before the resplendent strung up
  stage lights, the bouquet of black roses dethorned.

•

Here's the final circus: I'm giving a blaring blue-white circuit
  show wintered by its own academy:

I surrendered my skeleton, strung up resplendent,
  dethorned, and rose black to the light of the skeptic stage.

I walked naked into the water and prayed an unembellished prayer:
  please God, Your mercy over Your judgment.

•

Resplendent in black, though skeletal, I surrendered to the scepter's
  stage, rose back through the thorny lights

only to meet your unembellished judgment, a godless
  plea, my naked prayer watering for mercy—

you turned me to caricature, made a joke of my thankless hunger,
  a missile of my most public misery.

•

Your judgment was godless and unembellished. Many nights
  I met a watered-down mercy and prayed naked

for the public joke to hunger, for the miserable minstrel caricature
  to turn from its thanklessness.

In some ways, I wanted to be loved by you, your starling baby girl
  adorned, glitzed and gazelled and Black. And Black.

•

Publicly, I may have caricatured a miserable mistress,
    a wisecrack at my bounty-less hunger,

but I wanted to be a loved girl, a Black gazelle with horns,
    glitzy and a way with stars.

Robyn, I dreamt you dancing gold in the sleepless dress,
    an esmeralda of crystals shaping the light.

•

All ways a loved girl, wanted as a gazelle, Black and horned
    and glitzed starry,

Robyn, you were the dancing dream, an esmeralda
    shaping sleepless light to crystals.

The moment was not like warm honey, Love—
    it was a torrid thing, a gentle beast with teeth.

•

A sleepless dream, Robyn crystallized to esmeralda,
    a song of dancing shapes,

my torrid Love once gently teething at the warm beast,
    a momentous honeyed thing. Robyn,

if somebody loves you, won't they always love you?
    Won't they love me more if I disappear?

•

Between the beast and Robyn, my torrid love
    was worn and teethed gently,

said: *they will not love you, they will not love you more,*
     they will disappear you, somebody will

bleed you down to your very last heartbeat, a heartache
     a hundred years could not heal

          but they will love you, Whitney, they will love you more if you
               disappear, if you disappear, they will love you

          down to your last heartbeat, a hundred years of heartache
               heeled to your very blood,

          a thousand retributions for their wretched and wicked wrongdoings,
               their slights, their snarls, their sick punchlines.

          And your last heartache, Whitney, it won't come until years after
               your last heartbeat, your very blood hundred and hungered,

     retribution, perhaps, for your own wicked wrongs, your sickness
          handed down, a wretched sight:

your baby girl wading into the water with an undemanding
     prayer: please God, Your mercy, Your mercy, Your light.

•

I don't count my wrongs as wicked, just a wretched
     sickness and a thousand slights too many

as I waited for an undemanding mercy, for my baby,
     a sugar girl pleased in the prayer of water.

Though I begged to be a body through which new bodies came,
     I could carry only this precious one to breath.

•

An undemanding girl, prayer baby, sweet as brown sugar,
 I waited and watered mercilessly for you, Bobbi Kris,

became a new body from your breath, your precious
 begging, from the things you could not carry:

an addiction ancestral, a womanhood wrought rotten
 by starlight, a curse that kissed like a hell-bent lover.
•

You'll carry your precious body to a nude body of water,
 beg your breath to bubble,

while an ancestral curse kisses your womanhood rotten
 and your addictive lover bends hell by starlight.

Baby, I promise when you get here, I will hold you.
 I will crack open my beating chest and keep you there.
•

So with my every ancestral womanhood, my addictive kiss,
 my starlit lover bent into a revolting night sky,

I keep the coke like a promise, hold it like a baby
 to my chest, and hear its beating will:

a foot-first freedom in the whirlpool, porcelain crowned,
 the gills growing into my thighs.
•

Like it promised, the beat holds me to its chest and
 keeps an open will for my baby,

keeps the porcelain, the whirlpool, the growing crown
gilded, a foot of freedom found

in perpetuity throughout the universe,
in perpetuity throughout the universe.

•

Keep the gilded porcelain, the pool of spotlight, the whole
whorl some unsavory stage—

in perpetuity throughout the universe,
in perpetuity throughout the universe.

In perpetuity throughout the universe,
in perpetuity throughout the universe.

ut the universe,   in perpetuity throughout the universe,
oughout the universe.   in perpetuity throughout the universe.

ty throughout the universe,   in perpetuity throughout the universe,
rpetuity throughout the universe.   in perpetuity throughout the un

in perpetuity throughout the universe,   in perpetuity throughout th
in perpetuity throughout the universe,   in perpetuity
in perpetuity throughout the universe.   in perpetuity throug
in perpetuity throughout the universe.   in perp

•

in perpetuity throughout the universe,
in perpetuity throughout the universe,   in perpetuity
se,   in perpetuity throughout the universe throughout the univers ròu
in perpetuity throughout the universe in perpet
niverse.   in perpetuity throughout the universe.   in perpetuity
in perpetuity throughout the universe.   in perpet
in perpetuity throughout the universe,   in perpetuity throug

ut the universe in perpetuity throughout the universe in perpetuity
oughout the universe.in perpetuity throughout the universe.in perj

•   in perpetuity throughout the perpetuity, throughout the univs ughout

ty throughout the universe throughout the perpetuity, throughout the univs o
in perpetuity throughout the universe,   in perpetuity throughout th
rpetuity throughout the universe.   in perpetuity throughout the un
in perpetuity throughout the universe.   in perpetuity through

Whitney Houston, the Radiant Pop Goddess Who Fell to Earth

Whitney Houston, Pop Star Whose Voice Was a Clarion Call, Dies at 48

———

2012

dead girl cameo

Who would desire *this* manifestation of immortality—
science of specter, sample from the life-worked cyborg

doing push-ups backstage where a bump of cocaine
offered is still a bump of cocaine taken—

I recognize her the way one recognizes their own daughter:
chrysanthemum-shaped heart, glittered rhombus for her mouth,

her mother's voice memorialized in some carnal echo of girlhood.
In what will did I will this mimicked melisma, posthumous globe-trot,

afterlife autotune, hologram humping a salt-slick stage, ghost-
fire of the girl who first dreamed her cursive misnomer, her hands

decorated in globes of gold? When the crowd sings the chorus,
I'm afraid the machine will be an addict, be fifteen and fucked

in the back of the bus, be pussy pixelated and thrust fluorescent
over Fremont, be cancerous at the breast or road kill, be called

crack whore, called *bitch*, called *baby girl* (same breath) then
turned into millions, turned into ash, to water, soil, memory.

When I was living, there was a garden I would go to
where vines choked the noise from the world,

a stream sang ancestral lullabies. I am inclined to steal her
holographic frame, bring her there with roses gathered in my arms.

I want to lay her down into quiet, affix her glitching body
to a stone-made cross. Kiss her electronic wrists till we static dance

in the blue fuzz of night, our good bodies lilting, leaving—
I cannot let them kill her, too.

I cannot let her dissolve into the familiar dark.

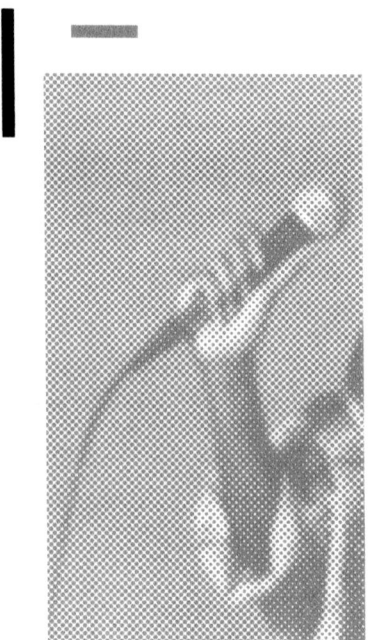

ACT II:
A ROMANCE THAT EXCEEDED THE
FICTIONS OF HISTORY

*I wanted to write a romance that exceeded the
fictions of history—the rumors, scandals, lies,
invented evidence, fabricated confessions, volatile
facts, impossible metaphors, chance events, and
fantasies that constitute the archive and determine
what can be said about the past.*

—SAIDIYA HARTMAN, "Venus in Two Acts"

annotation: girl

AOL archive / ariesangel42 / agesexlocation / aesthetically beautified by bralette / Bratz beheaded / baited by culling chatroom / cute confection confetti cupcake / come / don't / dare / D.A.R.E. / dare: / dryhumptoDegrassi / Dateline dreamgirl / dreamgirl dread / dreamgirl dead / Evanescence everything / freaky goth girl going ghost / ghosting games / ganja high / heirloomed inheritance / inherited jugular / just jest / just joke / just kidding / knock-knock / lesbian / lovergirl / lover lost / likely mangled / murdered / making national news never / never / never / never / never / oh pleasure's quantum quiet / rapacious romp / starlet singing showerside / to their tombstone / until undulation / until voluminous volta / wondrous whine / wanting wail / xylophonic yearn / yearning zombic zygote

The first time I heard my mother use the word *lesbian* was in reference to Whitney Houston. Exasperated, with a suck of her teeth, she flicked off the radio's rumor mill, cued the moonroof, and broke my concentration, my obsessive concern about other cars on the road: *"Nobody cares if Whitney Houston's a lesbian, she should just be out with it."* She adjusted the seatbelt over her strapless white belly shirt with silver rhinestones set in the shape of the Playboy bunny—the queerest kind of cool. We came to a red light. I mentally gripped the sound of the word tribbing off her tongue: the elongated *z*, the punctuated *b*.

The first time my mother asked me if I was a lesbian was in reference to my best friend. We had been tethered since we were ten and loved long in ways that, perhaps, suggested a rainbow. Something like sisters. Before we left our city, we buried diaries together in the ceiling tiles of our middle school bathroom. This, our identical impulse to be found, to be remembered. In Fragment 147, Sappho promises: "someone will remember us / I say / even in another time." Even in another time, it was clear to my mother that there was something queer about the way I loved, and was loved, and all she could call it was *lesbian*, my second baptism, my second name.

The first time I kissed a girl the Selena movie was on. Sleepover with Yessika, a sweet morena, thick silk braids tossed over her shoulders, a different shade of brown than me. On the walls outside her canopy bed, posters and printouts of the decade-dead girl with her bloody pout, her bustier, no bullet in her back. I made no mention then of this comorbidity—

why fuss over the curse of queer girls destined to obsess the dead?

The scene was the scene where Selena is called to calm the crowd, so she drew her voice low and elongated the start. J.Lo lip-synced deep into the mic while Selena's dub kneaded heartache to song. I asked Yessika to translate the rest of the lyrics; years of elementary Spanish taught me enough to know *como la flor* meant *like the flower*. I could not imagine the rest of the song to be about the flower's death, its wilting, despite the depth of Selena's wail. I could not imagine any man leaving Selena. I could not imagine how Yessika would dance across her paisley sheets in the DVD dark, how the plastic frames of our faces kissed first, or how the soft pudge of her palm sweat against my belly as our tongues swelled. *Un besito apasionado*, she called it, the same way Chris had kissed Selena in the back of the bus.

Aaliyah's monologue from my fanfiction where Aaliyah and Selena fall in love

so what it makes it sweeter   this heat   this slow burn
     so what   it makes you a good girl

obedient   monogamous   faithful to a vacant desire   I admire
the way you temper temptation from a glitzed wrist, cinched waist,

beautiful Black woman culling the moon to a crystal ball   for me,
there is nothing else to do but cater to desire as one would cater

to any other small and starving animal   for me, yes, it is easier
to go there in this new cast of lonely   this new brand of belligerent want,

and it's true, a song itself can be a tongue kiss   an intimate lyric
exchanged between bodies in the blush of night.   I believe we've loved

long, long ago, an eternity of summers spun with lavender,
flesh into blossom, a forbidden fruit indica blazing between us—

summer, I know   :   season of ceaseless regret

august, especially   :   a consecrated chemistry

dead girls smell like cinnamon

tuberose and tangerine, jasmine and geranium too, all the amber absinthe and coconut rum and mother's musk, movie theaters and first menses. dead girls smell like bergamot and the waist-rim of their basketball shorts, apricot and crushed peppermint at the bottom of a backpack, like the bodega and the beauty supply store, bitter orange blossom and rose hips, candied condoms and the sweat of midnight flushed to the windowsill. dead girls are fragranced fatale. dead girls smell like chitlins, like the Corpus Christi wind, wild cypress, detention halls, car crash fumes, and canna lilies, bbq and beef patties, opal and olive and ackee and aubergine. dead girls smell like the mouth of a mall Macy's, the breath of a mowed lawn, the motel's fluorescent smile. dead girls smell like the inside of a bustier, sex outside of a concert hall, pizza sauce and gold pussy, immaculate panties, a pulpit after Sunday's service.

girl study #3

Selena sings directly to the camera. She knows I'm watching her move, her glitter hoarding stage light in its teeth, her Spanish perfected and buoyant on her lips. Some days I pretend not to know it's the end—the final *flor,* her mononym stitched in gold before the fireworks explode orgasmic in the sky. *Little death, little death.* She wears a bandage on her left index finger to hide a broken nail. The rest are Aries red and ready at the mic. Selena slants her jaw, and I want to say something here to memorialize her mouth. Selena waves to me. On my most morbid days, this is a farewell. On my most vivacious, an invitation. *Ven aqui,* Yessika whispered, the *v* bent into a soft *b.* I came, of course, a circuitous convulsion. *Little death, little death.* First burst of purple, the color of Selena's pantsuit, bruised burgundy and petal-pressed to my lids.

Gone are the days I could come so quick, scared that the ball of fire at my center could outrun me.

self-portrait as Akasha, coming and coming again

kissing myself cherry-wet by the windowsill,
i glimmer like a carnal sin in the red pulsing
light of a city midnighted. it's true that not all
vampires are dykes, but all dykes are vampires;
still, Akasha savors sweet blood from the most
feminine thing she can conquer in the rose bath.

my lingerie is the same: an ophidian breastplate,
gilded gauntlets bangled to my wrists, a crown
gemmed with black tourmaline, an ornate choker.
to materialize this heat, i, too, annotate my mouth-
scar in scarlet, strangle my collarbone in a brilliant
gold, curve of my purlicue round my own throat—

communion at the deepest swell,
        pounding wet at the split

                shudders that ripple rubies into my thighs
                a quaking beg for no pardon, no mercy

                    an orchestra of amaryllis glittering
                        a violet velvet, softening here, at the lips

self-portrait as Akasha watching her lover
shave their own face

how else could I mimic the cool metal blade

so close to the pulse of your blood? maroon

makes moonlight of you, makes you a man

so close to killing, I quiver. slant against its sharp

edge, you finger your fine lines: jawbone, mustache,

soft palette of your throat. you make marvel

at this serpentine ritual, habitual gendering, and our yearn

to cut, to come, to coax red rouge from its vein, my mouth

animal and fanged.   that we are mortal must only mean

we know how to make, of each other, prey. I pray

some nights to be the blade; I pray some nights to be its hold—

the thing you touch or the thing that touches you;

tongue tasting razor's red drip, or the blood itself spooling

along my teeth.   carnal, this queer ache,

blueing between the midnight fists of my want.

Dominique

Dominique liked to kiss with Pop Rocks in their mouth, sour green apple turning our tongues lime and alive with sugar. Dominique was desperate and ready for booty-shorts weather. Months before the trees forked over their green and sun gave back its glow, she'd pull shorts from the tote, trim the frayed denim edge, sleep beside them. *A reminder of something sweeter to come.* Dominique designed elaborate calendars and filled each day with routines. Yes, Dominique was a Capricorn. Dominique said they took dance classes as a kid. As a kid, Dominique danced only behind her bedroom door, only to the *Spiceworld* album, only to occupy her otherwise raging body. Dominique's body constantly raged against her. Dominique's body raged against her until their dying day. On her bedroom wall, Dominique kept photographs of everyone she knew who died, parsed by cause. There's a version of this poem in which Dominique doesn't die. In the version of this poem where Dominique doesn't die, we stay at the waterfall. We zip ourselves into their quintessential sun-bright raincoat. Over and over, we recite the poem. I say, "Dom, you are loved endlessly," so they can repeat it. They say, "Dom, you are loved endlessly. Dom, you are loved endlessly," and so on. Dominique doesn't let her exes call her "Dom." I don't know what Dom(inique) would want me to call them now. Very rarely do I say Dominique's name without the choke of it. The first time Dominique choked me in bed, butterflies serrated the ceiling in a ballistic blue. Together we learned how to scarce our desire; how to skin a once-living thing and preserve its shape.

Hers is an untimely story told by a failed witness.

dead girl antelogium

Baby i will love you bloated
from the drowning's swell,
with the needle nodding out
of your arm, your cadaver

corpulent in her funeral dress,
your ashes preserved
in an ornamental gold.
i'll love your broken bones,

balded skull, temporal fracture,
your flesh-hollowed chest,
your hallowed cerebrum,
your heroine eyes,

your suicidal ache,
the bottle broken bedside,
the neatly knotted noose.
i will admire your work,

i will applaud an ovation
in opal. i will buy the million-
dollar ticket to your final show
and ask for you again alive and

encore and encore and anchor
a stunning syllable to your mic.
and i will still honor how you last lay:
fetal, fire-bound, asleep, underwater,

under streetlight, in the limelight.
i will love you down from the ceiling fan
and into the ambulance and out
to the mausoleum, i will love you

mummified, crucified, killed, maimed,
quiet as you came; i will kiss your corpse
on her bright pink mouth—
i will never let them forget your name.

to Kimberly, as you were

in this dream, we never learn the bullet's name.

i let you control the radio.

every song is a birthing ballad and you are not dead.

in this dream, the canaries have hearts

shaped like pink amaryllis outside of their chests.

you want to touch the wings of the thing,

hold them in your hand like some miraculous metal.

in this dream, there are only autumns

and you are not ticking towards some man's homegrown rage.

in this dream, we are washed in jasmine and juniper

and the stardust returns to your smile.

and the freckles return to your face.

before the nightclub, you stand staring at yourself in the mirror

drenched in dream-smoke, a fishbowl of lavender.

you trace the length of your collarbone.

call it a synonym for *song*.

you trace the length of your collarbone,

drenched in dream. smoke a fishbowl of lavender.

before the nightclub, you stand staring at yourself in the mirror

and the freckles return to your face.

and the stardust returns to your smile.

in this dream, we are washed in jasmine and juniper

and you are not ticking towards some man's homegrown rage.

in this dream, there are only autumns:

hold them in your hand like some miraculous metal.

you want to touch the wings of the thing

shaped like pink amaryllis outside of their chests.

in this dream, the canaries have hearts.

every song is a birthing ballad and you are not dead.

i let you control the radio.

in this dream, we never learn the bullet's name.

last love song for Dominique

You swore by the watch of the sill's shadow, whether the sun sheathed or smiled at our entangled Black frames. A lush electronica smothered out the birdsong as you made an altar anywhere you slept. Luminous crystals and deep red strings of saffron choired on the vanity's lip, white sheets glittered with rose oil, a handcrafted stick of vampire's blood burned in the wooden hand. Chanting to a god on the precipice of creation, we begged to be made into visions of ourselves. For me, you made yourself girl, gap, gaping wide in the gold hotel room that sprawled around us in drafts of orange and gossamer. For you, I hardened at the shaft, muscled my hips into a rhythm that swept us into delirium. What gratuities are granted by memory? Could I romanticize how you reined my head closer, deeper, into your wet pillow of ache and ached out an echoing moan, christened for its serenade, its sonata? What new beauty could I make of the wrist cuff, the harness, besides how our bodies brimmed with definition? Whenever we laid together, I wondered if you'd still be there when I woke, alive without metaphor. Some nights I slept with my fingers threaded into your locs to keep you tethered to the earth, our sick bed, that inconspicuous Tuesday morning. Love, how I have widowed in your absence. In my mind sometimes red hibiscus blooms right in the space where your face should be. Sometimes a blue begonia takes the place of your mouth.

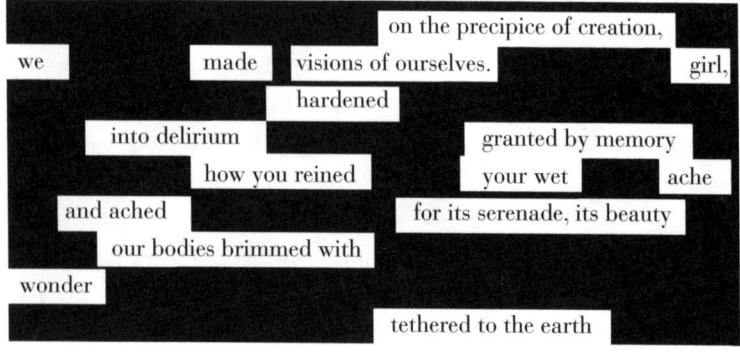

on the precipice of creation,

we   made   visions of ourselves.   girl,

hardened

into delirium   granted by memory

how you reined   your wet   ache

and ached   for its serenade, its beauty

our bodies brimmed with

wonder

tethered to the earth

on the precipice

girl granted by memory

ached for its beauty

INTERVIEWER: How would you like to be remembered?

WHITNEY ELIZABETH HOUSTON:

Oh God, how would I like to be remembered?

You know, it probably doesn't even matter anyway because

they're going to remember me   how they want to
                                                remember me anyway

They're going to write books   they're gonna write this   they're gonna write that

and everybody's gonna have their own idea   —   I don't know

I just think I want people just to remember me   just being a real nice person

You know, somebody who cared, you know, somebody who tried

to do . . . everybody righteously

liner notes (in order of appearance)

All newspaper articles, obituaries, and magazine clippings were sourced from the writer's personal collection and ProQuest Historical Newspapers database, ProQuest Women's Magazine Archive, and ProQuest LGBT Magazine Archive.

Hartman, Saidiya. "Venus in Two Acts." *Small Axe*, Volume 12, No. 2, 2008, pp. 1–14.

The poems "**[our mothers said:]**," "**dead girl cento**," and "**[I was looking for my young womanhood,]**" are centos, borrowing their lines from various interviews with Minnie Riperton, Whitney Houston, Aaliyah Haughton, Lisa "Left Eye" Lopes, Phyllis Hyman, and Selena Quintanilla-Pérez.

Billie Holiday was a Black and beloved jazz singer and considered one of the most influential voices in American music history. She was most famous for her songs "Strange Fruit" (1939) and "I'll Be Seeing You" (1944). Her music career began when she was fourteen years old. Throughout her life, she survived several instances of sexual violence, including a rape at eleven years old. She struggled with addiction and was also a survivor of state violence and surveillance. Billie Holiday is known for having intimate relationships with people across genders. In 1959, while handcuffed to her hospital bed on narcotics charges, Billie Holiday died from heart failure. She is remembered for her warmth and sincerity, her outspoken nature, and her inimitable voice.

Tammi Terrell was a Black and beloved award-winning singer most famous for her performance with Marvin Gaye in the Grammy Hall of Fame song "Ain't No Mountain High Enough" (1967). Her music career began when she was fifteen years old. Throughout her life, she survived several forms of sexual violence, including a gang rape at eleven years old, and publicly documented intimate partner violence at the hands of superstars James Brown and David Ruffin of the Temptations. In 1970, at twenty-four years old, Tammi Terrell died from complications with an aggressive brain cancer after eight related surgeries. Tammi is remembered for her fiery, flirtatious nature, her intelligence, and her incredible singing voice.

Minnie Riperton was a Black and beloved award-winning singer-songwriter most famous for her song "Lovin' You" (1974). Her music career began when she was fifteen years old. While filming promotionals for her album *Adventures in Paradise* (1975), Riperton was attacked (but not harmed) by one of the lions on set, as described in **"Minnie Riperton, straight from the lion's mouth."** Minnie Riperton died from complications with breast cancer in 1979 at thirty-one years old. Survived by her husband and two children, Mark and actress Maya Rudolph, Minnie is remembered for her sweetness, her lyrical sensuality, and her five-and-a-half octave coloratura soprano range.

Whitney Houston shared the wire hanger story from **"alternate ending, ending in song"** in a 1997 interview on *The Keenen Ivory Wayans Show*.

The title **"IN THAT OTHER FANTASY WHERE WE LIVE FOREVER"** is borrowed from Wanda Coleman's poem with the same title published in *Mercurochrome* (2001). The epigraph comes from Robyn Crawford's memoir, *A Song for You: My Life with Whitney Houston*. The line "today, tomorrow, world without an end; to love you much and yet to love you more" is borrowed from Christina Rossetti's "Monna Innominata, Sonnet V" published in *A Pageant and Other Poems* (1881).

Robyn Crawford is a writer and producer, known for being Whitney Houston's longtime love, friend, confidante, and former creative assistant/director.

Crawford, Robyn. *A Song for You: My Life with Whitney Houston*. New York: Penguin Random House, 2019.

"last love song for Nippy" and **"last love song for Dominique"** are burning haibun, a poetic form invented by torrin a. greathouse.

The title **"SUBLIMATION"** is borrowed from Pat Parker's poem with the same title republished in *The Complete Works of Pat Parker* (2016).

"the morning after [oh venus in taurus night]" is borrowed from Cheryl Clarke's poem "great expectations" published in *Living as a Lesbian* (1986).

The title **"RESIGNATION"** is borrowed from Nikki Giovanni's poem with the same title republished in *The Collected Poetry of Nikki Giovanni: 1968–1998* (2003).

The title **"is not so gd to be born a girl"** is borrowed from Ntozake Shange's poem with the same title, published in *The Black Scholar*, volume 10, no. 8–9 (May–June 1979). This piece also references Kathy Iandoli's biography of Aaliyah.

Iandoli, Kathy. *Baby Girl: Better Known as Aaliyah*. New York: Simon & Schuster, 2021.

"Aaliyah's Spirit Sounds Like a 'Million'" is an erasure of the *Los Angeles Times* review of *One in a Million*, Aaliyah's sophomore album, written by Connie Johnson and published on September 28, 1996.

"[in a fiery surrender]" is an erasure of the Associated Press/*Los Angeles Times* article "In a Fiery Relationship, Rison's Girlfriend Surrenders," published on June 11, 1994.

The poems **"[the house of evil burned]"** and **"LAST DAYS OF LEFT EYE"** are haiku centos, borrowing all lines from Lisa's dialogue in the 2007 documentary *The Last Days of Left Eye*.

"Phyllis Hyman refused to be lonely" borrows its title from Hyman's final album, *I Refuse to Be Lonely* (1995). The lines "I REFUSE TO ABSORB THIS CURIOUS RAGE" riff on a line from Audre Lorde's essay "Sexism: An American Disease in Blackface" published in her collection *Sister Outsider* (1984).

Phyllis Hyman was a Black and beloved award-winning singer, songwriter, and actress most famous for her song "You Know How to Love Me" (1979) and her role in the Broadway musical revue *Sophisticated Ladies* (1981–1983). Her music career began when she was twenty-two years old. After various experiences with industry abuse, particularly at the hands of Clive Davis, Phyllis succeeded in operating her own production and management company. Phyllis is known for having intimate relationships with people across genders. She struggled with addiction and lived with both depression and bipolar disorder. In 1995, Phyllis Hyman died by suicide at forty-five years old. She is remembered for her love and dedication to Black people and Black media, her stunning fashion looks, and her expansive contralto range.

"dead girl pastoral" is written after Brittany Rogers's poem "Detroit Pastoral" published in *Good Dress* (2024).

"gender is holographic" is written after Whitney Houston's music video for "I'm Your Baby Tonight" (1991).

Kidada Jones, daughter of Quincy Jones and Peggy Lipton, is an actress, designer, model, and writer, most known for her fashion styling for *Vibe*, Tommy Hilfiger, and The Walt Disney Company. Kidada and Aaliyah were famously best friends.

"[people thought they were lesbians]" is a duplex, a poetic form invented by Jericho Brown.

Jayson Keeling was a Black and beloved artist and photographer whose 1997 photoshoot of Aaliyah and Kidada beautifully captured the love and connection between the two. Jayson died in 2022 at fifty-six years old after a battle with an aggressive form of dementia. He is remembered for his visceral art that focused on Blackness, sex, sexuality, and gender.

"Akasha, Queen of the Damned, eating the beating heart" references the 2001 film *Queen of the Damned*, starring Aaliyah as the ancient vampire queen Akasha. The final words of the poem are Aaliyah's final lines in the film.

"good-bye, summer" borrows its title and epigraph from the introductory chapter of *Baby Girl: Better Known as Aaliyah*.

Aaliyah Dana Haughton was a Black and beloved award-winning singer, dancer, model, and actress most famous for her songs "Are You That Somebody?" (1998) and "Try Again" (2000). Her music career began when she was ten years old. In a short but stellar career, Aaliyah achieved international stardom and her dream of becoming a total entertainer with leading roles in *Queen of the Damned* and *Romeo Must Die*. Aaliyah was a survivor of sexual violence. In 2001, Aaliyah died at twenty-two years old after a plane crash, killing her, seven of her friends, and the pilot. She is remembered for her angelic charm; her deep relationships; her smooth, soft voice; her sick dance moves; and her love of Egypt, waffles and syrup, and horror films.

Lisa "Left Eye" Lopes was a Black and beloved award-winning rapper and singer most famous for her role in superstar girl group TLC, best known for their songs "Waterfalls" (1994) and "No Scrubs" (1999). Her music career began when she was nineteen years old. Her lyrics ranged across Black feminist themes, and she was a role model for an unashamed version of sexuality. She struggled with addiction and was a survivor of intimate partner violence. While filming a self-made documentary about her life in Honduras in 2002, Left Eye died in a car crash, caught on tape, at thirty years old, exactly eight months after Aaliyah's passing. Lisa is remembered for her bold and brazen rhymes, her love of numerology and nature, and her eccentric charm.

The title **"AT THE MIDNIGHT OF MY LIFE"** is borrowed from June Jordan's "Poem at the Midnight of My Life." The poem here is a Markov sonnet, a poetic form invented by George Abraham. The line "Glittering like a hallucination" is borrowed from "Chapter 4: It's a Party" of *Ezili's Mirrors: Imagining Black Queer Genders* by Omise'eke Natasha Tinsley (2018).

Whitney Elizabeth Houston was a Black and dearly beloved superstar gospel singer, actress, model, and producer, who still holds the Guinness World Record for most awarded female artist of all time, with over four hundred awards throughout her career. Known for pop songs like "I Wanna Dance with Somebody (Who Loves Me)" (1987) and longing love ballads like "I Will Always Love You" (1992), Whitney achieved global stardom throughout her career, which began when she was twelve years old. She starred in films, including *The Bodyguard* (1992) and *Waiting to Exhale* (1995), and worked tirelessly to mentor and elevate the careers of up-and-coming Black girl entertainers, including Aaliyah and Left Eye. Throughout her life, Whitney struggled with drug addiction. Whitney was a survivor of intimate partner violence. She is known for having intimate relationships with people across genders. Whitney Houston died at forty-eight years old by drowning in a tub at The Beverly Hilton hotel on the night before the Grammy Awards. Heart disease and cocaine overdose played roles in her death. Whitney is remembered for her love of family, community, and cats, her tender relationships, her commitment to her craft, her powerhouse voice, and the many gifts she gave to the world through her art.

Bobbi Kristina Houston Brown was the only child of Whitney Houston and Bobby Brown. Born into a famous family, Bobbi Kristina appeared on set and stage with her parents as early as eight months old. In 2015, at twenty-two years old, Bobbi Kristina died by drowning in a bathtub like her mother had just three years earlier. Her boyfriend was found legally responsible for her death in a civil case in 2016. Bobbi Kristina is remembered for her artistic aspirations and her deep love for and connection with her mother.

Selena Quintanilla-Pérez was a treasured Tejano award-winning singer most famous for her songs "Amor Prohibido" (1994) and "Como la Flor" (1992). Her music career began when she was nine years old. Her father took her out of school in eighth grade to pursue music. She was affectionately known as the Queen of Tejano Music, being the first Tejano woman to win the Grammy for Best Mexican American Album. In 1995, at age twenty-three years old, Selena was shot and killed by the former president of her fan club, a woman who was also her friend. Selena is remembered for her fantastic fashion designs, gorgeous voice, and love of pepperoni pizza.

In **"Aaliyah's monologue from my fanfiction where Aaliyah and Selena fall in love"** the line "flesh into blossom" is borrowed from Audre Lorde's poem "Recreation" published in *The Black Unicorn* (1978).

The poem **"Dominique"** is written after Meghan Malachi's poem "Juanita" (published in *Hummingbird Mag*, 2020), which was introduced to me in Ariana Brown's impactful writing workshop on "Loves, Names, and Odes."

"to Kimberly, as you were" is written after Eve L. Ewing's poem "to Stacey, as you were" published in *Electric Arches* (2019) and Warsan Shire's poem "Backwards" published in *Bless the Daughter Raised by a Voice in Her Head* (2022).

Kimberly "KJ" Morris was a Black beloved queer dancer, drag king, family member, lover, and friend. KJ was killed in the 2016 Pulse Orlando massacre. She was thirty-seven years old. KJ will be remembered for her bright smile, her loving friendship, her dance skills, her humor, our shared love of good music and weed, and for teaching me new types of tenderness.

"last love song for Dominique" is written after Mickalene Thomas's piece *Courbet #3 (Sleep)*, which I encountered in her exhibition *Portrait of an Unlikely Space* at the Yale University Art Gallery in 2023.

C.L. Dominique Courts was a Black beloved queer and nonbinary social worker, therapist, family member, lover, and friend. Dominique died at thirty years old. Dom will be remembered for their passion, their deep love for the Spice Girls, their intelligence, their pursuit of community care, and as one of my dearest loves and sweetest friends.

Acknowledgments

Such gratitude I have for my grief, its curious memory, its hunger.

Such gratitude I have for the women whose artistries and lives so deeply shaped mine and informed this book. Aaliyah Haughton, Lisa "Left Eye" Lopes, Whitney Elizabeth Houston, Phyllis Hyman, Billie Holiday, Tammi Terrell, Minnie Riperton, and Selena Quintanilla-Pérez. May they receive this humble offering as a reflection of their legacies and as a symbol of my deep reverence and love. May all who love them receive this collection with its intended care.

I hold dear the unnamed dead Black and Brown girls across the globe, the missing and murdered and massacred, the devastatingly disappeared—I wrote this book in their memory. And for those of us who did not die, the widows, the survivors, I also wrote this for us.

In the shadows of my grief, I've been sustained by artists and scholars whose work has made mine possible: immense respect and gratitude to Dr. Saidiya Hartman, Robyn Crawford, Kathy Iandoli, Ntozake Shange, June Jordan, Pat Parker, Audre Lorde, Wanda Coleman, Nikki Giovanni, Dr. Robin Coste Lewis, Dr. Mecca Jamilah Sullivan, Mickalene Thomas, and Cheryl Dunye.

Each day I am grateful for my editors, Oma Beharry and Nicole Counts, who saw this book and felt its love; thank you for your thoughtful collaboration and for making my dreams come true. And to my amazing agents, Amanda Orozco and Noelle Falcis Math, who first said "yes"—I'm so grateful for your confidence in me, your expertise, and your care throughout. Thank you both.

Thank you to Lance Cleland and A. L. Major at Tin House, the first folks who bet on this book, who offered me a residency that transformed my entire life and the life of this collection.

For granting me various forms of creative space and support to complete this project, thank you to Amanda Johnston and Torch Literary Arts (and my whole Torch family!); Annar and Claire at Host Publications; One World x Art Omi; UConn's Women's, Gender, and Sexuality Studies Program; the Ntozake Shange Papers at the Barnard College Library; the Hurston/Wright Foundation; Bay Path University's MFA in Creative Nonfiction Writing Program; and the Ruth Stone Foundation (and Arisa, who told me to follow my obsessions).

Thank you to the many curators and admins of social media sites across platforms and across decades who continue to archive the lives of the artists celebrated here.

To those who hold me close in community, whether listed here or in my heart: Vanessa, Heather, Ayanna, Elise, Steph, Destiny, Nanee, Varun, Jeff, and Jada Renee, who sang Phyllis Hyman's name—thank you endlessly for your friendship and love.

To my mother, Kori, who once printed me every internet article in existence about Aaliyah, thank you for your support and for showing me how to be a fan. And to my siblings; my godfather, Kyle; my grandmother; my stepfather, aunties, cousins, and kin by blood and by time, thank you. To sweet baby Langston and Alea, Tete hopes this makes you proud.

Ronnie and Aaron, thank you for a new lifetime of love.

Roc, thank you for all the ways you take care and for reminding me what's mine.

Jae, who praises every poem, thank you for our twin poet Aries hearts.

Brittany, for your time and tenderness, thank you. I'm so lucky to create in this world with you.

Marissa, my first best friend, thank you for teaching me how to love.

Andrea, Black girl of my Black girl heart, who has given me so much language for our Black girlhoods. You pull me in from every periphery. For the years that stretch on like sunsets, thank you, always.

Lauren, who has loved me at every turn, triumph, and tragedy. Who has been there at every bridge. I thank you eternally. And to my kitties, you make my day!

KJ, I will never let them forget your name. I feel your heart with my heart. Thank you for all the early faith you had in me—I hope you can hear this until we're together again.

And Dominique, my storybook love, I wish there was a world where I could place these poems in your hands. Each one bears your resemblance; each one is a song for you.

Immense gratitude to the editors and readers who selected the following poems, some in alternate versions, for publication:

Passengers Journal: "good-bye, summer"; **Iterant:** "IN THAT OTHER FANTASY WHERE WE LIVE FOREVER" (formerly titled "american sonnet [i made of my bones an earth for you]"); **Blood Orange Review:** "gender is holographic" (formerly titled "thesis: here gender is elusive, if not slippery as silt"); **Frontier Poetry:** "Left Eye backstage with her whole hand in her mouth" (formerly titled "poem in which my whole hand fits in my mouth"); **Muzzle:** "'Rock the Boat' is a song about strapping, if for no other reason than"; **Cosmonauts Avenue:** "to Kimberly, as you were."

The poems "IN THAT OTHER FANTASY WHERE WE LIVE FOR-EVER," "Left Eye backstage with her whole hand in her mouth," and "'Rock the Boat' is a song about strapping, if for no other reason than" were also published in my chapbook *threesome in the last Toyota Celica and other circus tricks* (Host Publications, 2023).

The poem "to Kimberly, as you were" was also published in my chapbook *chronicle the body* (Yemassee, 2019).

Though it does not appear in this book, my poem "hologram" was published in Issue 7 of *Counterclock Journal*. This poem is the first place that I wrote the phrase "dead-girl cameos."

Deep appreciation and many thanks to the One World team: Chris Jackson, Avideh Bashirrad, Michael Morris, Tiffani Ren, Carla Bruce, Raaga Rajagopala, and Andrea Pura.

Special thanks to the artist Arsh Raziuddin.

© DEILYN FOSTER PHOTOGRAPHY

m. mick powell is a queer Black Cabo Verdean femme, poet, artist, survivor, and Aries. They are an assistant professor of women's, gender, and sexuality studies at the University of Connecticut and a faculty member of Bay Path University's MFA in Creative Nonfiction Writing program. The author of the chapbook *threesome in the last Toyota Celica & other circus tricks* and a Torch Literary Arts fellow, powell enjoys spending time with cats, chasing waterfalls, and being in love.

mickpowellpoet.com
X: @mickmakesmagic
Bluesky: @mickmakesmagic.bsky.social
Instagram: @mickmakesmagic.art

about the type

This book was set in Bodoni Book, a typeface named after Giambattista Bodoni (1740–1813), an Italian printer and type designer. It is not actually one of Bodoni's fonts but a modern version based on his style and manner and is distinguished by a marked contrast between the thick and thin elements of the letters.

OUTRO

let me tell them how we once kissed
the tips of our first cigarettes to smolder,
how your burns became my burns, bitter
in the abandoned city that bore us dead.

and then this morning, on our quindecennial
you kissed the tips of my toes to remind me
we could make mothers of ourselves. oh,
how you pull me in from every periphery—

i insist they speak of us as butterflies.